Horse and Equestrian Sport

JOSÉE HERMSEN

REBO
PRODUCTIONS

© 1996 R&B, Lisse
© 1997 Published by Rebo Productions Ltd
Cover Design: Ton Wienbelt, The Netherlands
Illustrations: Rik Slinger
Photographic research: Expertext, Garderen
Translation: Saskia Barker for First Edition Translations Ltd, Great Britain
Typesetting: Hof&Land Typografie, The Netherlands

ISBN 1 901094 48 0

Contents

Preface

I have enjoyed writing this book very much indeed. Not everyone gets the chance to write about their hobby, so I grasped the opportunity with both hands. Not only was writing the book great fun, but getting the photographs was quite an adventure too. For days on end a photographer and I travelled around looking for the right pictures to go with the text. I ended up on an extended ramble through the world of the horse and equestrian sport. I visited picturesque spots in my immediate neighbourhood which I had not realized existed. There is even a herd of Przewalski's horses within a few miles of my house.

While taking the photographs for the different kinds of equestrian sport, I realized yet again how many competitions and events take place that are well worth a visit. Furthermore, I met people everywhere who were perfectly happy to be photographed with their horses - I appreciated greatly. Even those for whom my request came as a total surprise were happy to co-operate.

One of the chapters is intended as a manual for the keeping and care of the horse. I remember well the day my first horse arrived. What I did not know then and had to learn by asking questions and reading, has been my guide in writing this chapter.

In writing this book I hope not only that I have been able to provide all sorts of useful information, but that I have also managed to convey my love of horses and of equestrian sports.

Josée Hermsen

CHAPTER I

The history and appearance of the horse

The horse did not always look as it does today, and in the course of its history it has been used for a number of different purposes. This first chapter will deal not only with the development of the horse, but also with its physical appearance and senses.

Right: A Przewalski's horse

Below: The development of the horse (a, b, c)

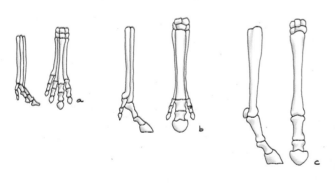

The development of the horse

Through the centuries the horse has changed a great deal. Research has shown that about 60 million years ago the horse was about the size of a dog (25-45cm, 10-18in high). It had four toes in front and three behind.

As a result of climatic change, the animal changed considerably. The horse's ancestor gradually developed from being a typical woodland animal, living as an omnivore in the tropical rainforests, to a vegetarian plain dweller. Because the animal used only its middle toe to run at speed over the plains, the outer toes of the fore and hind feet gradually reduced in size. The central digit in the front and back limbs developed into the hoof as we know it today. The horse also became much larger, and developed a larger brain and an entirely different jaw structure.

Two quite distinct types of prehistoric horse are thought to have been the ancestors of the breeds we know today. The Tarpan and Przewalski's horse are generally considered to be the ancestors of the Arab and other eastern breeds. These horses originated in the steppes and deserts of Central Asia. Their noblest descendant is the thoroughbred Arab, but many other lightweight breeds also share to a greater or lesser extent the blood of these steppe horses. They are grouped together as "warmbloods", a term that has nothing to do with the temperature of their blood, but is an indication that they are descendants of these eastern horses. The other group, known as cold-blooded, are the descendants of the heavily built horses that inhabited the forests of Central Europe.

This horse developed into the great medieval warhorse we know from paintings showing

Modern draught horses in a classic stable

An increasingly rare sight: a working horse pulling a milk cart

Recreational riding

them carrying knights in full armour. In turn, this noble animal contributed to the development of the modern heavy horses of Northern Europe.

The numerous different breeds we know today are the product of different combinations of these two groups.
The distinction between warm- and cold-blooded horses is minimal today, as many modern breeds have equal amounts of both in their veins.

The role of mankind

Man played an important role in the development of the horse.

From the moment that he saw the horse as a welcome aid in daily life, he used selective breeding to develop those characteristics which particularly suited his purposes.

In this way the horse developed into a draught, pack, or riding horse.

Over the last fifty years there have been further significant changes in the circumstances of the horse. Since the Second World War the increased mechanization of farming has meant a corresponding reduction in the use of horses. This was not good for the horse, but increasing mechanization also brought with it an increase in leisure time and a rapid growth in the use of the horse for sport and recreation.

1. forelock; 2. nose; 3. chin or curb groove; 4. throat;
5. shoulder; 6. point of shoulder; 7. breast; 8. forearm; 9. knee;
10. cannon bone; 11. pastern; 12. hoof; 13.(cushion of) heel;
14. ergot; 15. bulb of heel; 16. tendons; 17. elbow; 18. flank;
19. stifle; 20. gaskin; 21. chestnut; 22. hock; 23. point of hock;
24. hip joint; 25. root of tail; 26. croup; 27. point of hip;
28. loins; 29. back; 30. withers; 31. mane; 32. neck

The appearance of the horse

The horse's appearance is determined by its conformation, height, colour and markings. The sex and age also influence the animal's appearance. The demands we make of the horse's appearance depend on its breed and the purpose for which it is to be kept.

Conformation

It is very important that a horse should have the right proportions. The horse can be divided into

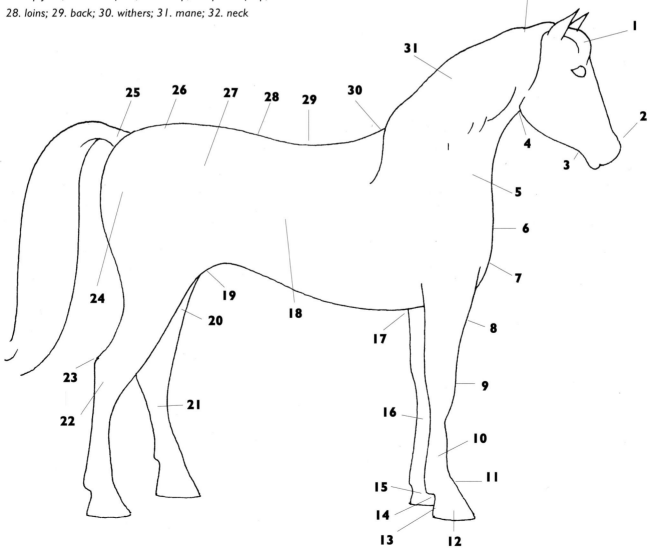

Above: Here the forehand, body, and quarters are easily distinguishable.

Right: Measuring a horse

forehand, body, and quarters. The horse's forehand is that part which lies in front of a rider and the saddle, the body is the middle portion, and the quarters are the hindmost part of the horse. The quarters are very important because they are, as it were, the horse's engine. The conformation, development and musculature of the quarters determine to a considerable degree the performance of the horse.

Height

To ascertain the height of a horse you will need a measuring stick. This is used to determine the distance from the ground to the highest point on the withers. The height of a horse is normally given in hands, a hand being four inches. For example, horses and ponies can take part in pony competitions as long as they are less than 14.2 hands high (without shoes). To measure the height of a horse, the horse must be on a flat surface and standing with its weight evenly distributed over all four legs. The horse is then standing "square."

Colour

A horse's colour is determined by the colour of its coat, in some cases modified by skin colour.

In the latter case there are numerous possible variations. In addition there are broken-coated horses known as coloured, "paint" or "pinto" in North America. The following are the most common colours:

- solid colours: grey, chestnut, black, brown, bay

Colours of a horse, from left to right, from below to above:
grey, liverchestnut, dun, blue roan,
chestnut, bay, dapple grey, red roan,
black, palomino, strawberry roan, piebald

A liver chestnut

- dapple grey, roan (blue, bay or red, strawberry or chestnut), dun, palomino, cream
- broken colours: piebald (black and white), skewbald (any other colour and white)

Markings

By markings are meant large or small areas of white on the head or legs.
The following facial markings are recognized:

1. small star; 2. small diamond-shaped star; 3. large star;
4. large diamond-shaped star; 5. crescent; 6. droplet-shaped
star; 7. short narrow stripe; 8. short stripe; 9. stripe; 10. blaze;
11. long narrow blaze; 12. white face; 13. blaze and snip;
14. crooked blaze covering right nostril; 15. white blaze and
mussel with dark snip on nose

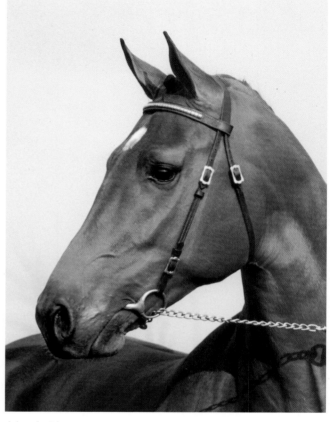

A head with a star

Different leg markings

Leg markings are distinguished as follows:

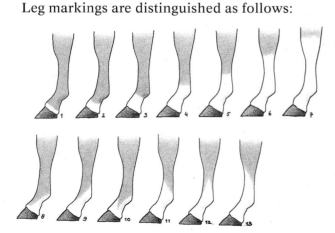

1. white coronet; 2. small sock; 3. sock; 4. white to one-third of
the cannon bone; 5. white to half of the cannon bone;
6. stocking; 7. white to over the knee; 8. white coronet
extending upwards at the back; 9. sock extending upwards at
the back; 10. sock extending upwards in front and behind;
11. half stocking extending upwards in front; 12. half stocking
extending halfway up the side of the cannon bone; 13. leg half
white to the front of the knee

Sex

Apart from their sex, mares and stallions also tend to be different in shape. Stallions are powerfully built and have a big crest along their neck. A stallion is usually more squarely built, the mare being more rectangular. Geldings (castrated stallions) are somewhere in between. Stallions are also different in character from mares. They are more alert to their environment and are frequently very energetic.

Age

The only way of being certain about the age of a horse is if its date of birth is given in a birth certificate or breed register. However, it is possible to guess the age of a horse reasonably accurately by looking at its teeth. For horses under five years the age can be ascertained by the disappearance of the milk teeth and the appearance of the molars. From six years old the amount of wear on the incisors in the lower jaw is the best guide to the age of the horse.

A three-month-old foal already has four incisors and four molars

The description

A detailed description of the horse is required for registration in the studbook or when a horse changes hands. The information given above may help you with this.

The senses of the horse

The horse needs its senses to react to events in its environment. The senses are as follows:
- sight (eye)
- hearing (ear)
- smell (nose)
- taste (tongue and roof of the mouth)
- touch (skin)

Sight

The horse sees the world differently from the way humans do. Because a horse's eyes are set in the sides of its head, it sees a different image with each eye, and can also see almost 360 degrees without moving its head. However,

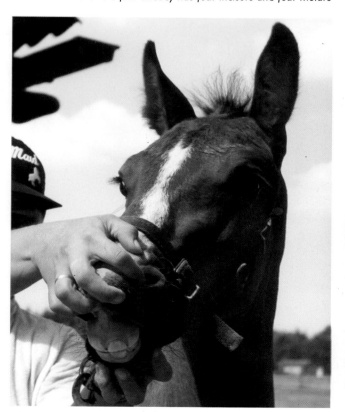

only a small part of this will be clearly in focus, and there is a blind spot immediately in front and immediately behind the horse. A person standing directly behind it cannot be seen by the horse. Diagonally behind, the horse will be aware of something but will need to turn its head to establish exactly what it is.

The horse can see things up to a distance of a few hundred yards. Anything beyond that, the horse perceives using its other senses. The horse has no depth of field, so it may be startled by a piece of paper or a shadow. When a horse shies, it is usually because it was unable to see something clearly. Do not punish it for this, but reassure it that there is nothing to be afraid of.

Hearing

The horse's hearing is many times more acute than that of humans. Its mobile ears constantly pick up all sorts of sounds from its environment. Experienced horse people can tell from

A horse's eyes are set in the side of its head

its ears what kind of mood the horse is in. Ears pricked forward indicate friendly interest. However, if the horse suddenly raises its head, tenses its neck muscles, and pricks its ears sharply, it has heard something which causes it alarm. If this happens, speak to the horse gently to soothe it. If the horse trusts you, it will soon relax. Be careful if its ears are laid flat back. This is usually an indication that the horse is angry.

Smell

Horses have a very sensitive sense of smell. For example, a horse can smell if there are other horses in the field. You may see a horse raise its nose and curl its upper lip if it has smelt something unusual. Stallions do this when they smell a mare.

Horses also use their sense of smell to judge their food and water. If they do not like the smell, they will not touch it.

Taste

Just like people, horses will like and dislike certain tastes. As a general rule, horses have a sweet tooth, but they will also lick at a salt block and will certainly not refuse sour apples. Their sense of taste also helps them to distinguish between poisonous and non-poisonous plants. For example, they will leave untouched the poisonous parts of buttercups.

Touch

A horse's sense of touch is very well developed – it can feel the slightest touch. A fly will be dislodged by the movement of muscles just under the skin. Horses also have long whiskers around their mouths, which they use to explore their surroundings.

Most horses like to be scratched, especially on the nose and under the chin.
Anyone who works a lot with horses needs to know how best to use these senses to their advantage. In this way it will not be hard to establish a good relationship with these sensi-

In this way horses demonstrate their affection for each other

tive animals. Never think of the horse as a machine that works the same way every day. One day the horse will feel more like working than another, and just like us it will prefer one person to another. Horses tend not to forget if they have been unjustly punished by someone. So always act reasonably towards your horse, and remember that it is a sensitive animal.

CHAPTER 2

The principal breeds and their characteristics

Purposeful breeding over centuries has resulted in the breeds we have today. In Europe alone there are 120 different breeds. Broadly speaking, equine breeds can be divided into the Arab, the English thoroughbred, warmbloods, trotting horses, coldblooded horses, and ponies.

Breeds have particular characteristics which distinguish them from each other. The English thoroughbred, for example, is known for its gallop, the Dutch draught horse for its strength, the Arab for its elegance, and the Hanoverian for its excellence as a riding and competition horse.

Friesians are known for their appearance at shows where they are harnessed to Friesian carriages and ridden by farmers and their wives in Friesian costume.

Royal Dutch warmblood

The modern Dutch warmblood was bred using Gelderland and Groningen foundation stock. The principal difference between the Groningen and the Gelderland lies in their paces. The Groningen has a good walk, a flat trot and a ponderous canter. The Gelderland is lighter in build and consequently has a lively elevated trot and a better canter. In order to develop a horse from this stock to meet the requirements of modern competition, the Groningen and Gelderland were crossed with, among others, the English thoroughbred, the Anglo-Norman trotter, the East Prussian, and the Holstein. The product of this breeding programme became the Royal Dutch warmblood. There are two distinct types of KWPN (Koninklijk Warmbloedpaard Nederland), namely the riding horse and the carriage horse.

Royal Dutch warmblood, riding type

American standardbred

American standardbred

The American standardbred is noted for its performance at the trot and is one of the fastest breeds in the world.

It is frequently seen at trotting races, where it performs well under saddle as well as harnessed to a sulky. A well-proportioned horse, it has a great deal of energy and endurance. Its height is 15 to 16.1 hands.

Fjord pony

The Fjord pony is distinguished by its cream or yellow colour, upright mane, and distinctive black stripe running from the forelock, along the mane and the back, to the tail. Originally the Fjord was a working horse for crofts and smallholdings. Today the Fjord is much in demand as a recreational horse, especially for waggon trips. It has a powerful walk and rather

Fjord pony

Holstein

a short trot stride. Average height is 13 to 14.2 hands.

Holstein

Originally the Holstein was a powerful, elegant carriage horse that could also be used under saddle.

The use of thoroughbred and East Prussian blood has refined the breed so that it now more closely resembles a riding horse. In harness and under saddle it has excellent manners and a faultless temperament. It has a long-striding walk, a roomy, powerful trot, an elastic canter,

and considerable jumping ability. Its height is from 15.3 to 16.2 hands.

Hanoverian

Hanoverian

The Hanoverian resembles in many respects the East Prussian. Like the East Prussian, it has a pleasant character and an even more equitable temperament.

It has rather more bone and, in general, a somewhat heavier build. It is an ideal riding and competition horse that can be used in various branches of equestrian sport. It has a

Following pages: The Brabant draught horse is an imposing animal of tremendous strength. Its ancestors were used for centuries as draught and farm horses in many countries of Europe. They are quiet, kind horses. The small head is in marked contrast to the heavy, muscular body. Its legs are short and are well feathered. This horse weighs between 750 and 1000 kilos. Its average height is 16.1 hands.

long-striding walk, an energetic trot and an elastic canter. Its height is from 15.3 to 16.2 hands.

Arab

The Arab is famous for its elegance and purity of blood. Many modern warmbloods are related to this breed – frequently via the English thoroughbred. As one might expect from an animal that has survived for hundreds of years in the desert, the Arab has considerable stamina and endurance. Its elegant movement is especially noticeable in the gallop. The head is the most characteristic feature of the Arab: fairly small with a broad forehead, narrow nose, the face being pronouncedly concave or dished. Its average height is 13.2 to 15 hands. Despite its well-muscled body, the Arab weighs not much more than 500 kilos.

Arab

English thoroughbred

The English thoroughbred is best known for its racing performance.
It can also be used for dressage, jumping, and hunting. It is a nobly built animal with a powerfully muscled body. On account of its conformation, it has a long-striding walk, a long low trot, and a tremendous gallop and jumping ability.

Only those horses whose lineage can be traced through the English General Stud Book can claim to be thoroughbreds. The thoroughbred is used all over the world to improve other breeds. Its height is up to 17 hands.

Shire

The most famous English draught horse is the Shire. Its height is 17.1 hands upwards and it weighs around 1200 kilos. The Shire has all the excellent qualities of a good draught horse, was much used in the past to work the land, and continues to be used by brewers to pull their drays.

English thoroughbred

Following pages: Shire horses harnessed to an historic mail coach

Lippizaner

The Lippizaner owes its fame to the Spanish Riding School in Vienna. Originally the breed comes from the borders of Yugoslavia and Austria. It is an intelligent breed that is eager to learn. It takes about seven years to train a horse for the haute Ècole.

Some Lippizaners continue to perform at a very high level until well over twenty years of age.

The elastic trot with its rounded action makes the breed particularly suited to advanced dressage.

The body with its heavy neck, rounded croup, and powerful shoulders is a model of strength. Grey is the most common colour. Its height is between 15 and 16 hands.

Below: Training a Lippizaner

Opposite: A Lippizaner performance

Hackney

The word Hackney is derived from the Middle English word "hakene" (lady's horse) which was used to distinguish it from the knight's horse and the war horse.

The Hackney is a trotting horse, though it is never used for trotting races. Valued for its remarkable action and build, it is a typical show horse. An elegant carriage horse, it is noted for its elevated paces, high head carriage, noble head, and high tail carriage.

Of all its paces the trot is particularly well developed, being very elevated in front. Its height is 14.3 to 15.3 hands, and up to 16 hands in America.

There is also a Hackney pony which has a maximum height of 14.2 hands.

Haflinger

The Haflinger is a modest, very strong mountain pony with great stamina. It has short legs and its back and quarters are well muscled. Notable is its powerful, broad croup. Its chestnut coat contrasts beautifully with its flaxen mane and tail.

The Haflinger is lively and has a good temperament which makes it pleasant to work with both in harness and under saddle.

Its height is about 14 hands.

Above: Hackney

Below: Haflinger

Right: New Forest pony

New Forest

The New Forest is used a great deal as a riding pony. It has good paces, and a good temperament. Its height is from 12 to 14.2 hands.

Shetland

The Shetland is the smallest pony and is principally used as a playmate for small children. Its height is 9 to 10 hands.

Welsh

The studbook classifies the Welsh pony according to size (sections A, B, C, and D). The original Welsh ponies are the small section A ponies. Those in sections B and C are typical riding ponies. Section B ponies have "foreign" blood; Arab blood particularly has been used to obtain the desired riding type. The horses and ponies in section D are Welsh Cobs, developed by cross-breeding with Andalusian horses imported in the Middle Ages.

Below: Shetland pony

Opposite: Welsh pony

Iceland

The Iceland, like the Haflinger, is a modest mountain pony with considerable stamina. In proportion it has a rather large head, a thickset body, and strong limbs. The Iceland is noted for pacing. Pacing is a form of trot whereby the laterals (right fore and right hind, and left fore and left hind) move forward together. Its height is between 12 and 13 hands.

Preceding page and below: Iceland ponies

Bottom: A magnificent sight: galloping horses

CHAPTER 3

The care of the horse

This chapter is intended for horse-lovers who keep one or more horses as a hobby. It will also give those who are thinking of buying a horse some idea of what will be involved in its care.

Shoeing a horse

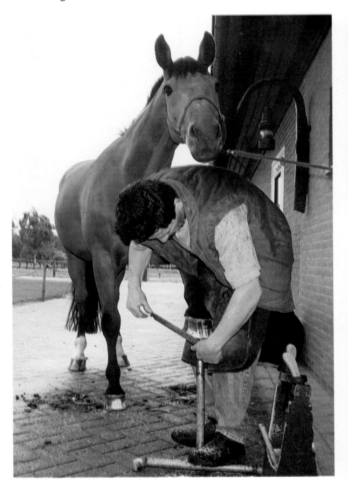

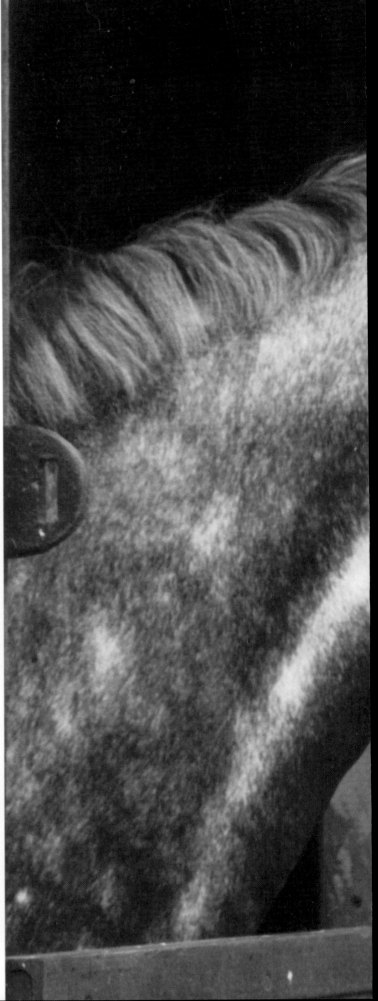

Introduction to horse management

In the winter, the care and riding of a horse will take an average of two hours a day. Added to this is the time needed for feeding, which should be done at least two or three times a day.

In the summer, if the horses are out at grass, they require less intensive care; the stable gets less dirty and a field with adequate grass provides enough food, especially for a pleasure horse. Furthermore, there is no need to ride the horse every day because it will already be getting plenty of fresh air outside.

In this chapter the following areas of horse management will be dealt with in succession: stabling, feeding, grooming, hoofcare, shoeing, trimming, and the use of rugs.

A stable door should be at least 1m (3ft) wide

Stabling

If you consider that during the winter a horse spends the greater part of every day in its stable, it is not hard to realize that the quality of stabling is very important.

A good stable must let in sufficient fresh air and plenty of light (it should not, however, be draughty), it should have a constant temperature of between 10 to 15 C (50º to 60º F), and be spacious and well built. To comply with these requirements the stable must have the right dimensions, be properly equipped, and be built of solid materials.

Dimensions

A stable should have certain minimum dimensions: at least 3.2m (10$^1/_2$ ft) high inside, but ideally even higher to improve ventilation, and

An insulating layer of bedding on a stable floor

at least 3m (10ft) square, with a door of no less than 1m (3ft) wide to ensure that the horse does not bang its hips when entering or leaving the box.

Equipment

The box will need a hay-rack, water bowl, and salt-lick. Nowadays hay-racks are fixed at chest height so that the horse can eat hay in a more natural position. Hard feed is given in a bowl that should be sufficiently deep to reduce wastage through spillage. A hatch or hole in the wall enables the horse to be fed without entering the box.

Automatic drinking bowls plumbed into the mains water supply require, of course, the least work. In winter you will need to make sure that the water in them does not freeze. A salt-lick

A salt-lick

ensures that the horse always has enough salt. Special salt-lick holders are available.

A high window is the best way of providing sufficient natural light. If this is not possible, then the window will need to be protected by bars to prevent the horse from breaking the glass with its head or legs.

A thick layer of bedding on the floor provides the horse with a dry place to lie down, as well as a layer of insulation between the cold stable floor and the horse. The most common forms of bedding are straw and wood shavings.

Construction

The walls and sides of the stable should be robust and smooth. Avoid sharp projections and edges, as the horse could injure itself on them. If wood is used for the construction, the boards used for lining the walls should be at least 4cm (1$^{1}/_{2}$ in) thick. If the walls are to be lined in brick, then you must use bricks and mortar that are tough enough to withstand a blow from a horse's hoof. In stables adjoining an internal passageway, the top of the wall could be replaced by bars from a height of 1.4-1.5m (4 $^{1}/_{2}$-5ft). The bars should be no more than 5cm (2in) apart, otherwise the horse could get its feet stuck between them.

The construction of the roof has a great influence on the quality of the ventilation in the stable. An old-fashioned pitched slate roof with a hayloft beneath is still the best. Corrugated iron is cheaper, but will require a layer of good insulation. Stables that are outside and have the top-door open most of the time should have an overhang with good guttering to prevent the rain coming in.

The floor of the stable is usually made of concrete. It should have drainage holes and should be on a slight incline to facilitate the drainage of water and urine. A thick bed and frequent mucking out will ensure that the animals do not end up standing in their own

urine and muck. There is no need to empty the whole box every day. What is important is to remove all the soiled bedding and to shake up the remaining bedding with a pitchfork. This is not an extravagance if you consider that a horse will do ten to twelve droppings a day, and produces some 7 litres ($1^1/_2$ gallons) of urine. Once a week you should clean out the whole box and put down a clean bed.

When building a stable, it is advisable to give some thought to the storage of feed, stable equipment and tack, as well as an area for grooming and washing the horse. Feed should always be stored in vermin-proof barrels or bins. Even if the horse gets out it should not be able to get to the feed bins.

Essential equipment for every stable are a pitch-fork, a fork, a shovel, a broom and a barrow.

Stable equipment

Feeding

The amount of feed that a horse needs will depend on its age, condition, and work. The nutritional requirements of a young, growing horse are different from those of an adult, and a pleasure horse needs less hard feed than a show-jumper travelling from one show to another.

Every horse requires the following:
(a) carbohydrates (starches and sugar), roughage, and fats
(b) protein
(c) vitamins and minerals.

Carbohydrates are necessary for energy. Proteins are important for the formation of muscles, hooves, coat, blood, milk, etc. Finally, minerals and fats help to build and maintain the bone structure and the proper functioning of the body.

Today a number of manufacturers will supply so-called pony nuts. Pony nuts are a ready-mixed feed that meets high scientific criteria in terms of their composition and nutritional value. They are easy to use and, if supplemented by hay and carrots for example, the horse will be getting an adequate basic ration. Do be careful to feed the right kind of nuts for your horse. If your intention is to go for a gentle hack through the woods twice a week, you do not want to feed your horse nuts designed for high-performance horses. The gentle hack could turn into something rather different. If you have only recently become the proud owner of a horse, you may ask yourself how many pony nuts your horse needs. The rule of thumb is 1 to 1.5 kilos of feed per 100 kilos of body weight. The following table is a rough guide to how much your horse or pony might weigh:

height	weight
up to 12hh	200-300kg
12-14hh	300-400kg
14-15hh	400-500kg
15-16hh	500-650kg

A horse may in principle eat hay all day.

These amounts are based on the horse being ridden for pleasure for about one hour a day. If it has a day off, you should give it less feed, and if it is in harder work then you will need to increase the amount or supplement its feed with oats.

A horse may, in principle, eat as much hay as it wants. Furthermore, hay will prevent the horse from getting bored during the hours it spends in its stable.

However, hay should always be good quality. A horse will avoid eating poor-quality hay unless it is very hungry. No one is a better judge of the quality of hay than a horse!

Water is the most important foodstuff; like humans, the horse can survive hunger better than thirst. Horses can be very fussy about the temperature and quality of their water. It should be around 10°C, fresh, and tasteless. If the water has a funny taste, a horse may refuse to drink it for as much as two days. As long as automatic drinking bowls are kept clean, they provide a continuous supply of fresh water which the animal can drink whenever it wants.

An appetite for pony nuts

How often and when should a horse be fed?
In the wild, horses eat continually with occasional short breaks. In this way they constantly take in small amounts, and this is what their small stomach was designed for. It is, of course, best to try to imitate this situation as much as possible.

However, it is scarcely practical to feed a horse ten times a day, and the horse also has to work. Feeding three times a day already goes a long way in the right direction. Two feeds a day is enough for a horse in light work, but do ensure that it also has sufficient hay to last the day. Hay is very filling and also gives the horse something to nibble.

Horses that work during the day should have their largest feed in the evening. Do try to keep to fixed feeding times. If you constantly change the times of feeds, your horse will become nervous and develop digestive problems. Make sure that food bowls are kept clean. Left-over feed that goes mouldy can be dangerous.

A horse in a field largely feeds itself. A field with enough good grass supplies most of the nutrition a horse needs. With its supple, mobile lips a horse can pick out exactly which grasses it wishes to eat. A horse will not eat grass that it does not like. Just look at the field! There will always be places where the horses do not graze.

Whether or not you will need to supplement the grazing with pony nuts or bran mashes will depend on the quality of the grazing, but particularly on the amount of work required of the horse. Bran mashes are made up of bran with boiled linseed, or linseed meal and boiling water.

Finally, be sure to make the transition from hard feed to grazing and vice versa gradually.

Grooming

Skincare is the main reason for grooming a horse. We sometimes think that a horse needs grooming only to look beautiful. Of course it is important that a horse should look its best, but its appearance is secondary.

The frequency and thoroughness with which a horse needs to be groomed depend both on the way in which the horse is kept and on the time of year. For example, a horse that spends much of its time in a field needs oils to protect it

Rolling in the field is good for the skin.

against the cold and the rain. Too much grooming would deprive such a horse of its natural protection against the weather. By rolling in the field, preferably in sand, the horse will ensure that its skin is massaged as necessary.

The stabled horse is a different case. You need to help the skin to function as well as possible. Daily grooming cleans and massages the skin. Excess oil, flakes of skin, dirt, dust, and dried sweat all need to be removed. If this is not done, then the pores may become blocked, and these are essential to regulate the horse's body temperature.

During the winter, horses (with a winter coat) need brushing with a dandy brush more than they do in the summer.

Grooming kit

To groom a horse you will need a metal, rubber, or plastic curry comb, a dandy brush, a body brush, a soft cloth, a mane comb and a sponge.

How should a horse be groomed?

You should first work over the horse's coat thoroughly with a curry comb in order to remove surface dirt and loose hair. This will accumulate in the teeth of the curry comb, so you will need to knock the comb on the ground occasionally to clean it. Always start grooming at the top of the neck on the near (left) side and work backwards with a circular motion. Then repeat on the off (right) side.

Then remove the loose dirt with the dandy brush before finishing the horse off with the body brush or cloth to produce that extra shine. Finally, use the dandy brush to remove dirt from the mane. The mane comb is used only to thin the mane, which is known as pulling the mane.

The tail should be brushed as little as possible. To avoid pulling out hairs unnecessarily, it is better to remove bits of straw by hand. If the

A mane comb, a metal, rubber or plastic curry comb, a dandy brush, a body brush, a woollen or towelling cloth, and a sponge

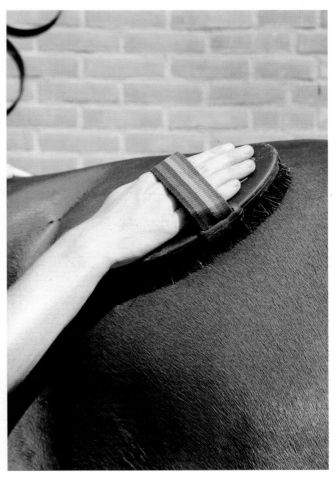

Finish the horse off with a body brush or cloth in order to bring out that extra shine

tail is really dirty, wash it in lukewarm water and soft soap or a special horse shampoo.

The sponge is needed in order to wipe the dust from the corners of the horse's eyes and from its nostrils after exercise. When grooming the quarters, never stand directly behind the horse. However trustworthy your horse is, it could still be startled by something and lash out backwards.

When should a horse be groomed?

The best time to groom a horse thoroughly is after exercise when the horse has dried off. Putting the horse away covered in dirt and dried sweat cannot be considered good skin care.

In the summer many horses enjoy being hosed down after exercise. Always start by hosing down the legs. Afterwards the horse can be dried off using a sweat scraper.

Hoofcare

To care for your horse's hoof you will need a hoof pick, a dandy brush, and a narrow paintbrush.

It is best to make a habit of picking out the horse's feet before and after exercise in order to check whether the horse has stepped on something sharp. If you were to realize this only after one or two days, a nasty infection could develop.

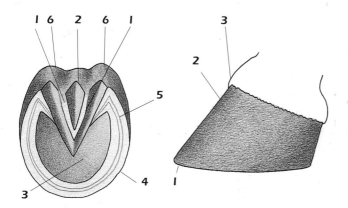

View of the hoof from below:
1. Cleft between frog and sole
2. Frog
3. Sole
4. Wall of hoof
5. White line
6. Bulb of heel

Side view of the hoof:
1. Load-bearing portion of foot
2. Wall of hoof
3. Coronet band

A hoof pick, a dandy brush, and a paintbrush

The sole of the foot must be scraped clean with the hoof pick. Special attention should be paid to the frog and to where the shoe meets the sole. To pick out the feet, always stand beside the horse and ask it with great confidence to lift the leg nearest to you. Horses are very sensitive to fear, and will not readily lift their legs if they sense uncertainty.

It is a good idea to clean the hoof thoroughly once a week. The whole hoof should be scrubbed clean with water and a dandy brush before oiling the wall of the hoof, the sole, and the coronet band to prevent the hoof drying out. Do be careful not to damage the coronet band when scrubbing with the dandy brush.

Once a week is, of course, just a guideline. As with grooming, the frequency with which the hoof need to be cleaned in this way will depend on how the horse is kept.

A horse that occasionally gets its feet wet will be less troubled with dry hoof than one which is permanently stabled and ridden only in an indoor school.

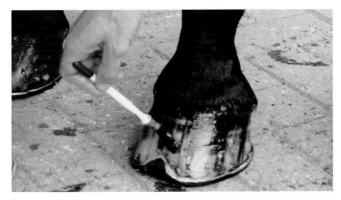

Oiling the hoof

Standing in its own muck and urine for long periods will tend to soften a horse's hoof. If the hoof are soft, regular applications of "brown tar" will improve them.

Shoeing

A horse that is hacked out regularly will need a new set of shoes every six to eight weeks. Horseshoes protect the wall of the foot which would otherwise be worn down on metalled roads more quickly than the horn can grow.

To shoe a horse you need horseshoes, horseshoe nails, special equipment, and . . .

a good farrier

A worn horseshoe

First of all the farrier removes the old shoes. He loosens the nails and . . .

pulls the shoe off

Then the hoof need to be trimmed

When a horse is shod, the hoof does not wear down naturally, so it needs to be shortened by the farrier and . . .

rasped

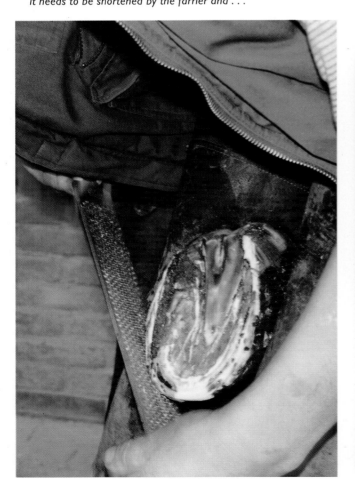

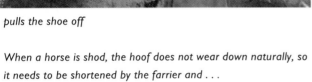

Then the shoes need to be shaped to fit the foot exactly.
To do this they are heated and beaten into shape

In order to fix the shoes in place, the farrier needs between six
and eight nails. These nails need to be driven into the white line.
If the farrier drove them in any deeper he would touch the
sensitive laminae of the foot and the horse would go lame. If the
nails were only in the outside of the hoof, they would have
insufficient purchase and the horse would quickly lose the shoe.

The nails should emerge about an inch above the bottom of the
foot. They are then cut off, leaving just a short length, the clench.
The clenches are then turned down and beaten into the wall of
the foot. The wall of the foot is then given a final rasp.

Only horses ridden exclusively on soft going can be ridden unshod.

Shoeing a horse is best left to a good farrier. If a horse is poorly shod it could go lame.

Trimming

Trimming is a kind of beauty treatment for the horse. Excess hair is removed and long hairs are trimmed.

The way a horse should be trimmed depends on its breed. For example, a riding horse is trimmed differently from a carriage horse. If you intend to take part in a competition or a show, it is as well to check with the relevant Breed Society how your horse should be trimmed.

For official competitions and shows, horses frequently need to have their manes plaited. In my experience it is impossible to learn how to plait from a book.

For official competitions or shows it is often necessary to plait the horse's mane.

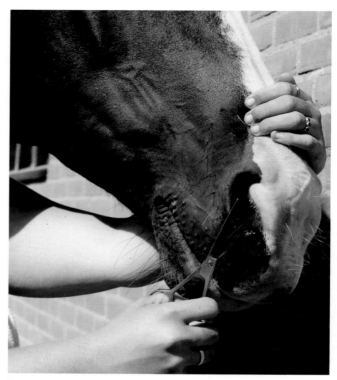

The whiskers around the eyes, lips, and nostrils should not be cut too short.

It is far better to ask someone who is good at it to show you how to do it.

Before trimming the horse, it should first be well groomed. There is also little point in trimming a horse before it has lost its winter coat.

The head

The hairs in the gullet need to be cut off using a curved pair of scissors with blunt ends. This special pair of scissors ensures that you will not accidentally injure the horse if it moves suddenly. These scissors can also be used to trim the long hairs protruding from the horse's ears. The hairs inside the ears should be left, as they protect them from cold, dust, and insects. The long whiskers around the eyes, lips, and nostrils should not be cut too short, as they are important feelers for the horse.

The mane

The mane and forelock need to be pulled using a mane comb. Always start at the ears and work in the direction of the withers. The correct

Here the mane has been hogged

length of the mane is approximately one hand's breadth. Take a small bunch of hairs that are too long and wind them once around the mane comb, then pull them out with a brisk down-

ward movement. As long as you always take small bunches of hairs, having its mane pulled will not be painful for the horse.

Manes are not always pulled; they may also be hogged (clipped). The mane is frequently also clipped behind the ears where the headband of the bridle goes.

The tail

The hair on the side of the tail may be cut, clipped, or pulled.

The tail should increase in size from top to bottom, and reach approximately halfway down the cannon bone. Some breeds have their tails "banged" (cut straight across), while others are left as a switch (ending in a natural point).

The legs

The hairs on the legs can be trimmed using scissors or clippers. Clippers or a razor can be used to trim the hairs at the coronet band.

The use of rugs

Most horses in work will be rugged when the temperature drops below 10°C (50°F). A rug not only keeps the horse warm but also prevents the winter coat from getting too thick. The disadvantage of a thick winter coat is that it can be almost impossible to get dry after exercise.

Of the many kinds of rugs available, you will need at least two: a stable rug and a sweat rug. The more expensive stable rugs are frequently made of canvas or nylon. My experience is that it is worth spending the extra money to buy a good stable rug, as a good-quality rug will last far longer. If you intend to use it as a New Zealand rug as well so the horse may roll in it in the field, a good-quality rug is essential.

Sweat rugs are used on horses that have sweated up during exercise. When the horse has dried off, it is exchanged for a stable rug.

The hair on the side of the tail may be cut, clipped, or pulled.

CHAPTER 4

Principles of horsemanship

This chapter focuses on the basic elements of riding such as mounting and dismounting, the acquisition of a good seat, and the giving of aids. The paces of the horse, saddlery, and riding in a school will also be discussed.

Right: A good seat is very important

Below: The hands are held closed, thumbs uppermost with the knuckels facing forwards, approximately a hand's breadth above the mane

Developing a sense of horsemanship

To learn to ride well, it is very important to have a good instructor: you cannot learn to ride simply by reading books about riding. You will also need a well-schooled horse on which to develop your sense of horsemanship. It is practically impossible to teach an inexperienced rider on an inexperienced horse.

Riding well depends on the correct timing of the aids. Aids are the signals the rider gives to the horse with the seat, legs, and hands that indicate the rider's wishes to the horse. By developing a sense of horsemanship, I mean learning to apply the aids correctly.

A good seat is essential, but before you can achieve that you need to be able to mount and dismount.

Mounting and dismounting

To mount a horse, stand on the near side with your back to the horse's head. Take the reins in your left hand and place your left foot in the stirrup. Grasp the front of the saddle with your right hand and swing your right leg over the back. Always lower yourself gently into the saddle: do not land in it with a thud! Always be careful to avoid prodding the horse with the toe of your left foot as you mount.

To dismount, first take both feet out of the stirrups. Then swing your right leg over the back of the saddle and slide gently to the ground. If you were to leave one foot in a stirrup while dismounting and the horse were to take fright and run away, your foot could easily remain caught in the stirrup and you could be dragged behind the horse.

The correct seat and position

A supple and independent seat is the foundation of riding well and the only position from which the aids can be given correctly. The rider must, as it were, sit "in" the horse and follow its movements with suppleness. To acquire a good seat, the beginner must do many sitting exercises. Lessons on the lunge are especially effective: the rider learns to remain in the correct position as the horse goes faster or slower. If you are able to follow the movements of the horse with suppleness, you will more easily be able to retain your balance. By tensing up or stiffening, you just work against the horse. Sitting "in" the horse, you will feel both seat bones in the deepest part of the saddle. Your loins and arms should remain supple, acting as shock absorbers so that you can keep your hands still. If, on the other hand, your every movement is transmitted through your hands, you will constantly interfere with the horse's mouth and there can be no question of good horsemanship. Close your hands and hold them, thumbs uppermost and knuckles pointing forwards, about a hand's breadth above the mane. Keep your wrists relaxed so that you can follow the movements of the horse's mouth. You will then be riding with still hands, that is to say with hands that maintain a consistent contact with the horse's mouth. There should be only light tension on the reins.

The correct position is upright with shoulders relaxed, back, and down. Your upper arms should hang loosely beside your body (your elbows should not stick out), so that your lower arms form, as it were, an extension of the reins.

Your thighs and knees should lie relaxed against the saddle. The position of the knee should never change, as it forms the basis of the position of the lower leg which is responsible for many of the driving aids. The lower leg hangs down on or just behind the girth. The ball of the foot rests in the stirrup, heels down, toes pointing forwards.

To dismount, take both feet out of the stirrups. Swing your right leg over the back of the saddle and slide gently to the ground

The length of the stirrup leathers is very important for your position on the horse. To begin with, the stirrup leathers should be approximately the length of your outstretched arm. The length is then adjusted from the saddle when you can determine exactly how high the stirrup needs to be, and therefore how long the leathers need to be. The stirrup should be about an inch higher than the heel of your boot when your leg hangs relaxed.

Having read this description of the correct position and seat, you will understand that it can only be acquired with the help of a good instructor and by dint of much practice. So if you would like to learn to ride well, you will need to devote some time to it. Once you are sitting correctly, you can focus on the aids.

The aids

The aids are divided into weight, leg, and rein aids.

Leg aids

To teach a horse to move away from the leg, you can use a stick. If the horse does not react immediately to pressure from the leg, repeat the leg aid and touch the horse simultaneously with the stick.

It is important that a horse learns to react promptly to lightly given aids. To support your leg aids you can also use spurs, but you should

The rider's weight can be of considerable assistance in steering the horse

not ride with spurs before you are fully in control of your lower leg.

Rein aids

The reins are the means by which the indications from your hands are transmitted to the horse via the bit. To give good rein aids you need to maintain a light and elastic contact with the horse's mouth by keeping your elbows, wrists, and fingers relaxed. In downwards transitions to a slower pace or to halt, your hands resist the horse's forward motion. Rein aids are always given in combination with other aids. For example, to make a transition to halt, you drive the horse forwards into the transition while resisting with your hands. Never just pull on the reins!

Weight aids

The rider's weight can be of considerable assistance in steering the horse. For example, by shifting your weight to your left seat bone and putting greater pressure on the left stirrup, you indicate to the horse to turn left. Weight aids frequently support the leg and rein aids. They are also important in the transition to halt: by sitting deeply in the saddle you indicate to the horse that it should slow down.

Aids should never contradict each other. To go forwards, for example, you first drive the horse on with the leg, then give with the hands to enable the horse to go forwards.

The paces

The paces of the horse are walk, trot, and canter.

The walk

There is an old proverb which says: "By the quality of the horse's walk you can recognize the rider." To get the horse to move forward well in the walk, you need quite a lot of experience.

To walk forwards, the leg and weight aids are given at the same time as giving with the hands.

The walk

In the walk, the horse moves its legs in the following sequence: near hind, near fore, off hind, off fore. This is called lateral movement, that is, the pairs of legs on the same side move together. By pressing your leg behind the girth at the moment that the hind leg on that side begins to move forwards, you can increase the scope of the stride. The trick is then to ensure that every stride of the walk remains true and regular.

The trot

In the trot, diagonal pairs of legs leave the ground, swing forwards, and come down together. For example, starting with the near hind, the sequence is: near hind and off fore, moment of suspension, off hind with near fore.

The aids for the trot are basically the same as for the walk, but stronger. By driving the horse forwards rhythmically with your seat and legs, you determine the pace of the trot.

The trot can be ridden either sitting or rising (also known as posting). In sitting trot, you remain sitting in the saddle and by bending and stretching your loins you endeavour to follow the horse's movement. In rising trot, you rise out of the saddle at the moment the horse lifts one of its hind legs.

When doing rising trot in a school, you should leave the saddle when the horse lifts the inside hind. This is known as rising on the correct diagonal. To see whether you are rising on the

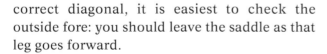

Rising trot (above and below)   *Canter right (above) and canter left (below)*

correct diagonal, it is easiest to check the outside fore: you should leave the saddle as that leg goes forward.

Canter

The canter consists of a series of separate leaps. To assist its balance on turns, a horse can canter on the right or on the left leg.

In right canter, the sequence of legs is as follows: near hind, off hind and near fore together, off fore, moment of suspension. In left canter the sequence is reversed.

In canter, the horse's whole body is used for balance. In order to be one with the movement, the rider must be balanced as well.
To be balanced, hold your upper body upright by allowing your loins to follow every movement. At every canter stride, the loins are

first rounded and then hollowed. The most important aid for canter is the seat. Your weight must be on the inside seat bone. By tensing your pelvic floor muscles, your seat is pushed forwards.

The inside leg remains on the girth, the outside leg is placed behind the girth. As the horse's body moves against your inside leg, you drive the horse forwards into canter with your right leg and your seat. As the horse lifts itself into the first stride, the reins give a little. It is very important that the seat, inside leg, and outside hand work together harmoniously.

It is best to ask for canter in a corner, because then it is more difficult for the horse to strike off on the wrong leg. A canter stride is about thirteen feet long, and the average speed of a cantering horse is twelve to thirteen miles per hour.

Saddlery

Saddlery, or tack as it is more commonly called in riding circles, includes everything used in the harnessing or caparisoning of a horse. I will restrict myself here to the two most frequently used items, the saddle and the bridle.

The bridle

The bridle consists of a number of straps that are fitted to the horse's head, a pair of reins, and a bit.

A bridle with a thick snaffle bit and drop noseband is the most usual. The thicker the snaffle, the more gentle its action on the horse's mouth. Only experienced riders on well-trained horses that respond to the lightest of aids, should use more severe bits.

The reins are attached to the bit, so that the rider can affect the sensitive areas of the horse's mouth. In this way he can direct the horse. There are two main types of reins: those for dressage and those for jumping.

Reins for dressage are completely smooth, while reins for jumping are not, thereby improving their grip.

Reins for jumping (above) and for dressage (below)

Below: Bridle with flash noseband

1. snaffle bit; 2. reins; 3. cheek piece; 4. drop noseband with 5. nose piece and 6. chin-strap; 7. throat lash; 8. head piece; 9. browband

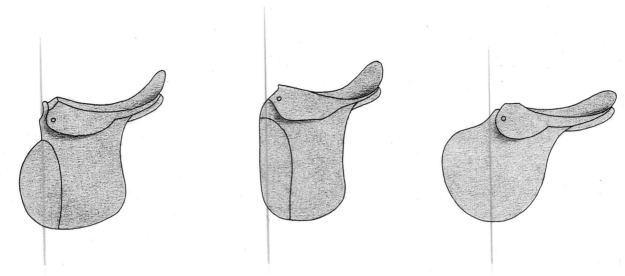

Left: general-purpose saddle; centre: dressage saddle;
right: jumping saddle

The saddle

There are various kinds of saddles. Those illustrated above are the most common.

Riding-school horses usually carry a general-purpose saddle which can be used in the school as well as out on a hack.

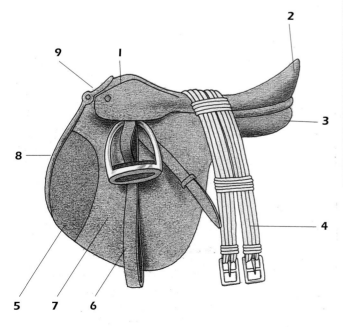

Numnah

A saddle cloth is usually placed under the saddle. Saddle cloths can be in the shape of the saddle (numnahs) or rectangular. The saddle cloth under a dressage saddle should always be straight in front.

Do not forget to clean all leather items of tack occasionally with saddle soap. After cleaning you should oil them thoroughly. To clean all the parts of a piece of tack, you will need to take it apart.

The general-purpose saddle:
1. pommel; 2. cantle; 3. cushions; 4. girth; 5. stirrup iron;
6. stirrup leather; 7. sweat flap; 8. knee rolls; 9. gullet

The riding school and school figures

A riding school has two short sides and two long sides; it measures 20x40m or 20x60m. The area just inside the boundaries of the school is called the (outside) track.

There is another track approximately 2m (6ft) inside the boundaries called the inside track. The side of the horse nearest the middle of the school is known as the inside. We distinguish the inside and outside rein, the inside and outside leg, etc. in the same way. If you are riding to the right, you are on the right leg or the right rein. There are letters at various points around the school.

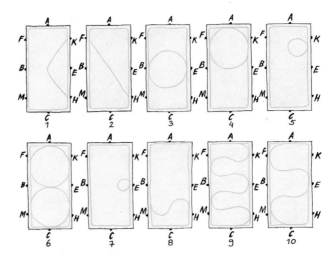

Grand volte at A (4); grand volte at B or E (3); 20m figure of eight at A or C (6); volte (5); volte at E (7); changing the rein by means of the figure S (8); three-loop serpentine (10); five-loop serpentine (9); half diagonal to X returning to the track before the corner (1); changing the rein (across the diagonal) from F or H (2)

By riding all sorts of school figures you can discover whether you are "steering" your horse correctly with your aids. In addition, the riding of school figures is useful gymnastic exercise for the horse.

The rules of the riding school

If several people are using the school at the same time, they will need to take account of each other. There are a few rules that you should always obey:

- If people are riding on both reins, those on the left rein always have precedence.
- The outside track is, as it were, the "main road" of the school. If you ride slowly on it, you hold up everyone else. If, for example, you wish to let your horse walk on a long rein during a session, do this on the inside track.
- Finally, never ride too close to another horse.

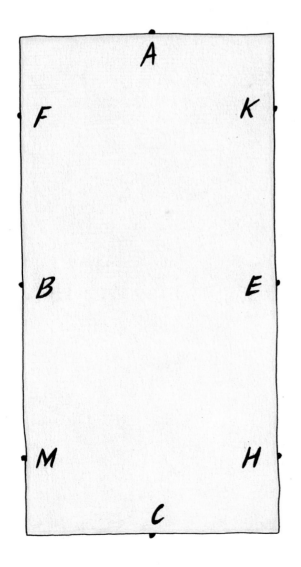

The centre of the line from A to C is known as X. These letters make it possible to ride school figures

CHAPTER 5

Training the young horse

Before a horse can be ridden it has to be trained. This chapter will deal with how to prepare the young horse to carry a rider on the lunge, and how it is broken in to the saddle.

Right: Lunging with a snaffle bridle

Below: It is a good idea to accustom foals to wearing a halter from the start

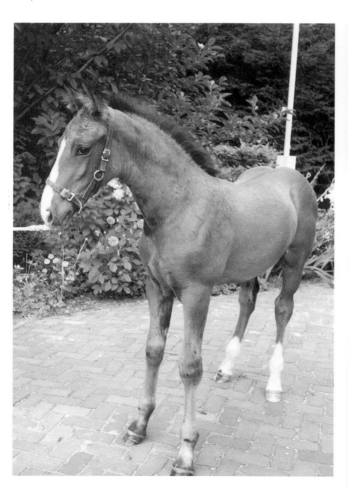

Training

The famous animal psychologist Von Maday once remarked: "If we want to have well-mannered horses we must be well mannered ourselves." By this he meant that a good horse trainer must have a great deal of experience, patience, skill, and self-control. If a horse is broken in correctly, there is no need for any violence.

The training of a young horse starts with the foal, by teaching it to have confidence in humans. It is a good idea to accustom a foal to wearing a halter from early on and to take it for a walk occasionally. In this way it will learn to be led willingly.

When the horse is two years old, you can start lunging it carefully. Lunging is when the horse, attached to a long rein (the lunge-rein), is made to move in circles around the trainer. The advantage of lunging is that the horse can learn to react to the aids and becomes accustomed to the girth, saddle, and bit.

How to hold the lunging rein

Learning to handle the lunging rein and whip

To lunge well, you need to be able to handle the lunge-rein and the whip. The lunge-rein should be looped in your hand without twists, and the whip should be held so that it points to the horse's quarters. The whip is not for hitting the horse, but for giving it signals. The horse must learn to trust the whip. The trainer should always keep the horse between hand and whip. The lunge-rein acts as a rein and should be kept taut by driving the horse forwards with the whip. The whip also prevents the horse from falling in on the circle. When lunging on the left rein, when the horse moves from right to left from the trainer's point of view, the lunge-rein

Preceding page: It is also a good idea to take a foal for a walk occasionall.

should be in your left hand and the whip in your right. When the horse is on the right rein, lunge-rein and whip change hands. In order to accustom a horse to the lunge, it is a good idea to enlist the help of a second person who can teach the horse to keep to the circle and obey the voice aids.

Never lunge for too long: the horse should find it enjoyable, and lunging can damage the joints of a young horse.

Voice aids

The horse must become accustomed to voice aids as well as those of the rein and whip. From the way the commands are given, the horse must learn to distinguish between commands to slow down or halt and to go faster. The former

A lunging cavesson

Boots and leg bandages

are given slowly in a low tone of voice ("whoa-aa"). Commands for an increase in pace need to be said in a more lively tone ("trot-on, canter"). It is important always to use the same commands and to give them in the same way.

Use of special equipment

It is a good idea to start lunging using a cavesson. This is a kind of bridle without reins or bit. There are rings on the noseband of the cavesson for attaching the lunge-rein.

To protect the horse against possible injury, you can bandage its legs. Working constantly on a circle, there is a greater chance of the horse striking itself than when working in a straight line. When the horse is familiar with a number of aids, you can lunge it using a snaffle bridle.

Never attach the lunge-rein only to the inside ring of the snaffle - you could easily pull the bit through the horse's mouth.

You can attach the lunge-rein by threading the end of the rein under the chin-strap, through the outside bit ring, before attaching it to the rein itself. Alternatively, you can thread the rein through the inside ring of the bit, attaching it to the outside ring. To avoid the reins of the bridle coming over the horse's head, twist them together, holding them in place with the throat lash.

Breaking in to the saddle

To accustom the horse to carry weight on its back, first lunge the horse using a breaking

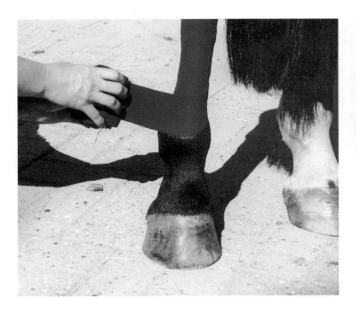

Bandaging a horse's leg for protection

*In order to accustom a horse to the lunge, it is a good idea to
enlist the help of a second person*

*The end of the lunge-rein has been passed under the chin-strap,
through the bit ring and then attached to the rein.*
*The reins have been twisted together and bound up with the
throat lash*

Above: Lunging with a lunging cavesson

Left: The lunge-rein has been passed through the inside bit ring and attached to the outside ring of the bit

roller. Once the horse is used to this, carefully place a saddle on its back.

It is best to put a saddle on the horse for the first time in the familiar surroundings of its own stable, and to have the assistance of a second person. The assistant can soothe the horse while the saddle is placed on its back and later when the girth is tightened.

Once the horse is accustomed to the saddle, it can be lunged with it on.

When the horse has become accustomed to being lunged under saddle, it can gradually become used to the weight of a rider. By this

Lunging with a saddle

Right: The horse must gradually become accustomed to carrying weight on its back

time the horse is at least three years old. The first time the rider should only lie across the saddle, patting the horse all the time.

When the horse is thoroughly used to all this, it is ready to be mounted for the first time. This is best done in a corner of the school where the horse cannot suddenly leap away. On leaving the corner, the assistant should remain slightly in front of the horse. It is quite normal for a horse to try to resort to flight when mounted for the first time. Only rarely will it really try to dislodge the rider. It simply reacts instinctively to a new situation. Once the horse realizes that the rider remains in place and that there is no danger, it should quickly stop bucking.

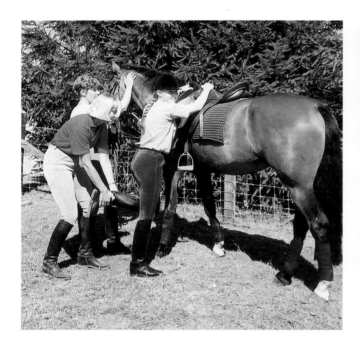

The rider stands close to the horse, the reins and a handful of mane in her left hand. She places her right hand on the pommel and the assistant gives her a leg-up

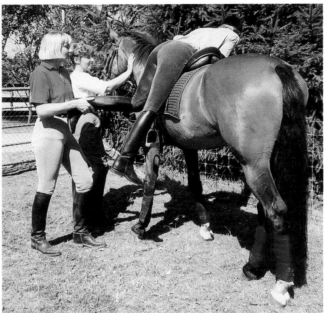

The rider carefully places her left foot in the stirrup

Quietly, but without hesitation, the rider jumps up and places her full weight on the saddle

She swings her left leg over, being careful not to touch the horse's croup

Keep the first lesson with a rider short. The horse should retain pleasant memories of it, and the best reward it can be given is to be allowed to go back into its stable or the field. It is a good idea to end the lesson by mounting and dismounting the horse several times with the assistant's help. By the third day it should be possible to mount using the stirrups. From

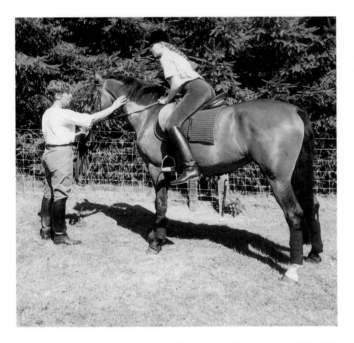

To dismount, first take your left foot out of the stirrup. This will ensure that if the horse is startled you will not end up hanging from the stirrup

to walk and trot steadily while the rider carefully takes up the reins. To teach the horse the driving aids, the trainer's commands should be accompanied by the rider's leg aids.

The horse should be introduced to the bit gently, as a young animal's mouth is very sensitive. If you taught the horse to halt on the lunge using voice aids, you should initially also use your voice to halt the horse under saddle. In this way you will scarcely need to use the reins at all to begin with. Finally, the best way of teaching a young horse to be ridden off the lunge is in the company of an older, experienced horse.

the beginning, the horse should be taught to stand still to be mounted and dismounted. It should remain standing still until the rider asks it to go forward.

I should emphasize that learning to train a young horse requires a lot of practical experience. If you have never done it before, you should enlist the help of someone more experienced. A badly trained horse will suffer the consequences throughout its life. On the other hand, a well-trained horse will enjoy being ridden much more and will give its rider much more pleasure.

Being ridden
The rudiments of being ridden can best be taught on the lunge. The trainer asks the horse

The rudiments of being ridden are taught on the lunge

CHAPTER 6

Dressage

Dressage is an important branch of equestrian sport. In dressage, you learn how to make a horse move as well as possible. By doing dressage, the horse learns to develop its natural movements and capacities further. A horse that is going well is well balanced and relaxed. It looks as though it performs all the movements of its own volition.

Conditions for good dressage

In order for a horse to move in a balanced and relaxed way, apparently of its own will, it must first learn to obey the rider's aids. In Chapter 4 we saw that a correct and supple seat is essential in order to give the aids correctly. Only when the rider can adjust his balance to that of the horse, will the horse be able to become supple, agile, and lively in its movements. The rider who takes account of the nature and character of his horse, and does not treat it like a machine, will have the greatest chance of success.

Impulsion, collection, and riding on the bit

Dressage is a matter of teamwork between horse and rider. The concepts of impulsion, collection, and riding on the bit are very important in dressage. The following paragraphs give definitions of these terms.

Impulsion

In dressage, impulsion is very important. Impulsion is the urge to go forward, created by the rider and wholly under the rider's control. Riding with impulsion is possible only if the driving and rein aids are well co-ordinated. When riding with impulsion, the lively desire to move forwards is not translated into a faster pace; rather the quarters are, as it were, driven further under the horse.

Collection

To enable a horse to move in a well-balanced way, we must teach it to distribute its weight correctly. In its natural state, the horse's forehand carries more weight than its quarters. When the rider's weight is added, the difference becomes even greater. By developing the muscles in the horse's back and quarters, we can enable the quarters to take over some of the weight carried by the forehand. In this way it is possible to restore the natural balance of the

Riding with impulsion

horse which was disturbed by the addition of the rider's weight on the forehand.

The term collection is used when the rider, by means of impulsion, causes more weight to be carried by the quarters.

Riding on the bit

Getting the horse on the bit depends on the co-ordination of the driving aids, and sensitive hands.

The rider should feel in his hands the impulsion created by the driving aids transmitted via the horse's mouth. You can see and feel that a horse is on the bit when its poll is relaxed, its neck curved, and there is gentle tension on the reins. The horse should not try to evade the action of the aids in any way.

Riding on the bit

Exercises

Now that we know roughly what a horse should look like when it is going well, the following are some exercises which function as a kind of gymnastic practice for the horse, and also help the rider to teach the horse to obey the aids.

Transitions

Work on transitions helps the horse's quarters to develop. A transition is the change from a slow pace to a faster one and vice versa. Transitions can also be made within the same pace, for example from trot to extended trot and back.

To go more slowly, the rider uses half-halts. In a half-halt the horse is driven forwards with the

seat and legs into hands that resist initially before giving way. A half-halt is a success if the quarters engage more, carrying more weight. The horse can be made to shorten its stride, slow down, or make a transition to a slower pace. It can also be asked to halt, or move backwards. A halt brings the horse to a stop. To go backwards, the rider begins by asking the horse to go forwards. As the hind leg comes up to go forwards, the rider asks the horse to go back by resisting with his hands.

To go faster, the rider must drive forwards with his legs and give with his hands. By "giving" we mean that, immediately after the legs drive the horse forwards, the hands allow the forward movement.

Riding curves and straight lines

Alternating between riding on a circle and a straight line is a good exercise for making a horse supple. To ride a circle correctly the horse must be in the following position: it should look in the direction that it is going, and should be bent according to the curve of the circle on which it is travelling. The quarters should follow in the same track as the forehand.

Rein back

The rider, too, always looks in the direction he is going, and by lengthening the inside of his body, places his weight over his inside seat bone. The inside leg drives the horse forwards and prevents the horse falling in. The outside leg is placed behind the girth to avoid the quarters swinging out, ensuring that the horse remains bent on the circle. Both hands are carried a little to the inside and forwards, but not to the extent that the outside hand crosses over the mane.

Never ride the same circle more than two or three times consecutively; alternate this exercise with that of riding straight forwards, for example, before repeating the exercise on the other rein.

Every horse is inclined to go crooked because it has a convex and a concave side. To make sure that the horse moves forwards straight, the rider must maintain the urge to go forwards (impulsion) and make sure that there is the same pressure on both reins. The horse will be inclined to lean on the bit on its convex side. If the rider correspondingly increases the pressure of the leg on that side, the horse will gradually begin to go more straight.

Lateral movements

When the horse has mastered the movements described above, you can introduce lateral work. In lateral movements, the horse moves forwards and sideways with the forehand and the quarters on different tracks. The object of these movements is also to increase the horse's suppleness.

Lateral movements include shoulder-in, quarters-in (travers), and half-pass. In shoulder-in, the horse moves on three tracks, bent away from the direction of travel. The quarters remain on the track while the forehand is brought slightly to the inside. The outside front

Top left: Riding a curve

Bottom left: Riding a straight line

Opposite: Half-pass

leg and the inside hind leg should be on the same track.

Quarters-in is a movement on four tracks, and the horse looks in the direction of travel. The forehand remains on the track, while the quarters are brought in. The half-pass is an advanced dressage movement in which the horse moves in a forwards and sideways direction. The forehand is led forwards by the reins while the quarters move sideways away from the leg. Other advanced dressage movements are passage and piaffe. Passage is a highly collected trot with a markedly elevated forehand and lowered quarters. Piaffe is a collected trot on the spot.

Competition riding

Competitions test the rider's control of the horse and his ability to perform the required movements accurately.

Quarters-in

Passage

Opposite: Piaffe

Dressage tests
Dressage tests are divided into short movements, each of which is awarded marks

Halt

If you frequently go to competitions, purchase a trailer

between 0 and 10. The manner in which the movement is performed determines to a great extent the marks awarded.

Judges look to see whether the required movement is performed at the stipulated marker, not before or after it, whether the horse negotiates the corners without loss of rhythm, cutting the corners, or reduced impulsion, and whether the circles are round and of the required size.

Dressage tests are divided into classes according to the experience and ability of the horse. A combination of horse and rider will normally start to compete in the lowest class, moving on to the next class as they are awarded points for their performance in competitions.

Required dress

Those wishing to take part in competitions must realize that they and their horse will need to be well turned out. In some countries a mark is even awarded for turn-out. The horse must be well groomed and the rider must wear the correct clothing. In the dressage arena the correct turn-out for the rider is:

• black or dark blue riding jacket
• white, beige, or yellow jodhpurs
• matching white or yellow tie or stock

• gloves
• black riding boots
• riding hat, top hat, or bowler

In the lower dressage classes the use of spurs and a whip is permitted. In the higher classes, the use of a whip is forbidden and spurs are compulsory.

When riding in a competition, bear in mind that the most important thing at all levels is the total harmony of horse and rider.

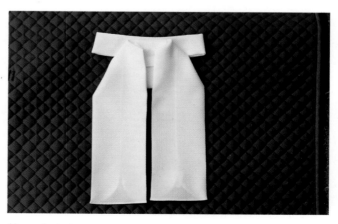

Above: A stock
Opposite: Horse and rider ready for the show

CHAPTER 7

Showjumping

Most horses jump enthusiastically and well without a rider. The problems occur when they have to retain their balance with a rider on their back. A horse can jump well only if there is good co-operation between horse and rider, and the horse is troubled as little as possible by the weight of the rider.

The moment of suspension

The horse's jump

If you study the movements of a horse jumping by itself without a rider, you will observe that it approaches the obstacle at a constant speed and takes off in the right place. To determine its take-off, the horse lowers its head and neck. At take-off, the horse raises its neck and places its hind legs far under its body. Then it lifts its forehand and stretches its hind legs to push off from the ground. While suspended over the obstacle, it again stretches its head and neck forward. The movements of the head and neck have an important function in jumping. On landing, the horse raises its neck.

The fore legs reach the ground first, and the hind legs are placed almost in the hoof-prints of the fore legs as canter is resumed. It can be seen from this description that good balance is essential for jumping. The rider will need to ensure that, even with an extra weight on its back, the horse is able to maintain its balance.

When the horse takes off from the ground, the rider should move his weight forwards slightly and follow the movement of the horse. His arms and hands follow the horse's head as it stretches its neck. The rider should maintain a light contact with the horse's mouth. During the moment of suspension, the rider prepares himself for landing. He should keep looking forward; if he looks down he will get behind the movement.

On landing, he must avoid falling heavily back into the saddle. As the horse's legs touch the ground, the horse raises its neck. The rider should ride the horse forwards actively as soon as the horse's hind legs touch the ground.

Preparing to jump

To jump well, and to be able to influence the horse, a rider will first have to develop an independent seat.

A good exercise for this is riding over cavalletti. The rider will also have to develop jumping sense in order to present the horse at a fence at the best place for take-off.

Jumping position

In order to enable the horse to jump with the least effort and the best balance, the rider must learn to keep his weight as still as possible in relation to the horse's centre of gravity. He must be able to sit still without using the reins in order to maintain his balance. The correct leg and rein aids can be given only from a completely balanced position.

The correct position for jumping is called the jumping position. To achieve this, the stirrup leathers are shortened by two or three holes so that the rider's knees come closer into the saddle.

The rider's upper body is bent forwards slightly and his weight is transmitted to the stirrups by means of his thighs and knees, thereby taking weight off the horse's back. It is important for the rider to keep his heels well down, so that his lower legs remain still. His upper arms should be relaxed, and his lower arms should act as extensions of the reins. The hands must follow every movement of the horse's head and neck.

Cavalletti work

A good exercise for developing the jumping position is work over cavalletti. Cavalletti

Jumping position

Start with one cavalletto

Cavalletti work

(singular: cavalletto) are wooden poles attached to a cross at each end at a height of 15-30cm (6-12in). By riding over four to six cavalletti placed at specific distances, the horse learns to move in a balanced way with a rider on its back and to judge distances.

The distances between the cavalletti depend on the size of the horse and its length of stride, and can vary between 1m (3ft) and 1.4m ($4^1/2$ ft). The first time a horse or rider works with cavalletti, it is a good idea to begin with a single cavalletto and to increase the number gradually.

Jumping sense

By jumping sense we mean the rider's ability to present the horse at a jump in the best place for take-off.

Jumping sense is very important

If the rider takes off too close or underneath a fence, the horse is likely to knock it down with its front legs.
If the rider takes off too soon, the horse's hind legs will hit the fence.

Knowing the right way to approach a fence and the best pace at which to do so is a skill that is hard to learn. Some riders have a better "eye" for a fence than others, and some horses are better at determining the take-off point than others.

Jumping sense can be developed only by jumping a great deal. A novice rider will need to learn to jump on an experienced horse. He should let the horse take the initiative and try to learn from every jump.
Conversely, a young horse is best taught to jump by an experienced rider. If such a rider presents the horse at a fence at the right pace and without interfering with it, the horse will jump well almost every time.

Take-off

Following pages: Landing

Kinds of fence

In addition to single fences there are also combination fences, which consist of two, three, or more elements. A triple, for example, consists of three jumps that are counted as one fence. The distances between the jumps are chosen so that one or two canter strides are necessary between landing and taking off for the next jump. Combination fences are given only one number, the different elements of which are identified by letters (A, B, C). If, for example, a horse refuses at C, then the whole combination must be attempted again.

The two principal types of single fence are the upright and the spread fence (or oxer). An upright can consist of a number of planks or

A triple

A gate and poles

A wall

An oxer

The ground-line enables the horse to determine the height and the take-off

The ditch

poles, a gate, or a wall made of blocks. When jumping uprights, it is important for the horse that there be a good ground-line because it can see only a limited amount of the obstacle from a distance of 4m (13ft). A ground-line makes it easier for the horse to determine the height and

Opposite: The arms and hands follow the horse's head

Jumping the wall in a puissance competition

Horses that tuck their legs up high when jumping usually wear a stomach protector

the take-off. Spread fences include various kinds of oxer, the triple bar (three poles at increasing heights), and the ditch. To jump an oxer, the horse must clear not only a given height but also a certain width. Ditches are usually 2-4m (6-12ft) wide and about 15cm (6in) deep.

Riding showjumping competitions

Showjumping competitions take place all year round. The competitions are divided into differ-

ent classes of increasing difficulty. Just as in dressage, by gaining points for the horse's performance, a rider can move up to a higher class.

Competitions are broadly divided into those in which speed is of the essence and those in which clearing the fences is more important. The latter are tests of jumping skill, and faults at fences are the deciding factor. If several riders have a clear round or the same number of faults, they will jump-off against the clock over a shortened course.

Walking the course

Horse and rider in perfect harmony

The rider with the fewest faults and the fastest time is the winner. Puissance competitions usually consist of several jump-offs. In these competitions the test is to keep jumping clear rounds over courses that get bigger at every jump-off. In the final round the wall can reach 2.25m (6ft 10in).

Usually a puissance lasts four rounds. If two or more competitors have jumped clear, then they share the prize.

Dress

Just as in a dressage competition, the rider, the horse, and the tack must be clean and well turned out.

The rider must wear boots, jodhpurs, shirt, tie or stock, and riding hat. In very hot weather the judges may rule that there is no need to wear a jacket.

However, even in very hot weather riders may not compete in T-shirts, jumpers, or sleeveless polo-shirts. In bad weather the judges may permit the wearing of raincoats.

The use of spurs and sticks is permitted in all classes. However, the whip may not exceed 75cm (30in) in length.

CHAPTER 8

Driving

Driving is the control of horses and ponies harnessed to a carriage or piece of horse-drawn equipment. The driver, also known as the coachman or whip, sits on the box in the carriage. The driver therefore can rely only on the reins, whip and voice, whereas the rider also has the use of leg and weight aids. Much driving nowadays is for recreational purposes; horses are used less and less for work.

Driving technique

When starting to drive, it is advisable first to practise the various hand positions in a "dry run." You can do this with a piece of equipment especially made for practising driving.

This consists of a plank of wood with two holes through which are threaded two pieces of cord about 1m (3ft) long. At one end of each piece of cord a weight is suspended, and at the other end the cord is attached to one of a pair of snaffle reins. The plank is fixed to the wall. The novice whip can then concentrate exclusively on handling the ribbons (reins).

When practising in this way it is a good idea to wear gloves and carry a whip.

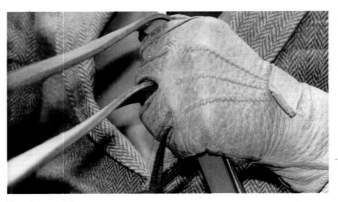

Starting position

Normal position

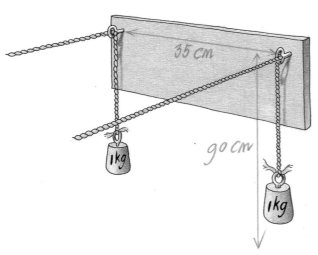

Weights for practising driving

Training position

Position at rest

The basic position for holding the reins is to hold both reins in your left hand, with the smooth side of the reins uppermost. The near rein should lie over the forefinger, and the off rein between the middle finger and the ring finger.

The lower two fingers grip both reins. Your left hand, lightly bent at the wrist, is held at the middle of the body. The whip is carried in the

Little finger strap

right hand. This is the position to which you will need to return after taking up any other position.

Normal position

The position of the left hand remains unchanged. Bring your right hand in front of your left hand and grip the off rein with the lower three fingers. The thumb and forefinger of your right hand rest on the near rein and point towards your left shoulder. Both hands are held upright in front of the body. The whip is held between thumb and forefinger.

Training position

To make the transition from the usual position to the training position, draw the off rein out of your left hand and about 10cm (4in) sideways

Mount from the near side and keep your face and left leg towards the horse

to the right. The distance between your hands and the horse's mouth must remain constant.

Little finger strap

The little finger of the left hand should always be looped through the strap at the end of the near rein where it is buckled to the off rein. This is to prevent the ends of the reins dragging on the ground.

Taking up the reins and mounting

Always start by making sure that the reins are the right length, so that you will hardly have to adjust them once you are on the box. Keep a light feel on the horse's mouth throughout.

Normally you mount the box from the near side. Stand with your left leg and face turned towards the horse. Keep an eye on the horse as you mount. The horse should not move forwards before you have given the aids with voice or whip to do so.

Slowing down and halting

To slow down, shorten the reins, by a few centimetres (an inch or two). From the normal position, place your right hand slightly further forwards; follow this with your left hand and grip with both hands. Repeat this as necessary until the reins are short enough.

To stop completely, you also start from the normal position. Place your right hand about 25cm (10in) in front of the left hand, and grip the reins. Then draw your right hand back. To make way for the right hand, the left hand is lifted straight up.

To extend the reins again, the right hand draws them slowly out of the left hand before going back to the normal position.

Going forwards

To give the horse the office to start, feel the horse's mouth gently and speak to him. Drop your hand as soon as the horse starts to move. If the horse does not respond to the voice aid,

Above: Moving off

Left: A left turn by giving with the outside rein according to the Achenbach system

touch him gently with the whip. The whip is primarily to give the horse directions, not to beat him!

The Achenbach system

A popular system of driving today is the Achenbach system, named after the German whip Benno von Achenbach who developed it. According to this system, all turns are made by giving with the outside reins rather than by shortening the inside reins.

Both reins are held in the left hand so that the right hand is free to use the whip or give direction signals.

Driving harness

The bridle of a carriage horse consists of head-piece, browband, rosettes, cheekpieces, blinkers, throat lash, noseband, Liverpool bit, curb chain, and reins. A Liverpool bit with a curb chain is the bit most often used for driving. There are three different positions for the reins to be attached to the bit.

The harness consists of: reins, breast plate, pair of shafts, girth, traces, collar, terrets, breeching strap, and crupper.

Above right: Bridle: headpiece, browband, cheekpieces, blinkers, throat lash, noseband, Liverpool bit, curb chain, reins

Below: With a saddle horse the harness can be laid out in readiness and wheeled over to the horse

Below right: Quick release pin. In an emergency, the pin can be removed quickly and easily, thereby freeing the horse

Driving competitions

There are competitions for singles, pairs, tandems (two horses harnessed one behind the other), and teams (four in hand).

The dressage test

Driving a dressage test can be compared to a test under saddle. A test consists of a number of elements which are judged separately, and every driving test starts and finishes with a salute. At the end of a test, a male competitor comes to a halt in front of the judges and doffs his hat with his right hand. A female competitor lifts her right hand, carrying the whip vertically to the right, and bows her head.

The obstacle course

The obedience of the horse and skill of the whip are tested on the obstacle course, which consists of a number of obstacles that must be negotiated in a particular sequence.

Each obstacle consists of two plastic or rubber cones with a ball on top which falls off if the cone is touched. The course must be completed in a given time.

If more than one whip completes the course without penalty within the time, there is a "drive-off" for first place. At the start of the competition, competitors are given the chance to walk the course, as they are in showjumping.

The correct dress for driving competitions

In a driving competition, men wear a dark suit and tie, and a bowler, or other felt hat. Women wear a suit, preferably with a long skirt, or a blouse and long skirt, with an appropriate hat.

Both ladies and gentlemen must wear gloves and a driving apron. The apron, which must fit snugly over the driver's lap, is intended to prevent the reins and gloves from staining the driver's clothing. These clothes are not compul-

Right: The obstacle course

Above: The whip halts in front of the jury and doffs his hat with his right hand

Preceding page: A tandem

Dress and carriage are colour co-ordinated

sory: you may also wear ordinary riding clothes or the livery of the association.

Some whips are beautifully turned out for competition, frequently co-ordinating the colours of their clothing with those of their carriage.

Other kinds of driving

There are two other kinds of driving competition: horse-driving trials and showing classes. Straightforward recreational driving is engaged in for pleasure rather than competition.

Horse-driving trials

These competitions are a spectacular sight for the public, involving cross-country driving which tests the training and obstacle-negotiating skills in difficult terrain.

On the box beside the whip sits a member of the jury, who accompanies the competitor throughout the competition and keeps a note of penalty points. The competitions for teams are especially popular with spectators.

Showing

In driving show classes the quality of the turn-out is judged, especially the appearance and movement of the horse. The quality of the trot is particularly important.

Opposite page: Horse-driving trials, testing the dressage and obstacle-negotiating skills under difficult circumstances

Showing (above) and driving for pleasure (right)

Driving for pleasure

Recreational driving through the countryside is
the most popular form of driving. Driving clubs
frequently organize tours, and those taking part
often dress up in period costume.

CHAPTER 9

Western riding

Today more and more riders are realizing how enjoyable and relaxed western riding and dealing with a western-trained horse can be. Those who wish to compete can choose between in-hand showing classes, classes under saddle, races, and working classes.

Right and below: More and more riders are discovering how enjoyable and relaxed western riding can be

History of western riding

Western-style riding developed in North America during the nineteenth century with the growth of cattle-ranching. The cattle on the large ranches had to be counted, branded, herded, etc., all of which was done by a number of men on horses.

It quickly became clear how important it was to have supple, agile horses with a calm, willing character. In addition, the horse had to be ridden with one hand so that the cowboy could work with the other. The usefulness of a cowboy depended largely on the ability of his horse. A cowboy often depended on his animal

The colour of this Quarter horse is described as blue roan

day and night. Force and fear were therefore too dangerous as training methods.

The first essential was a calm, relaxed horse capable of thinking with and for the rider. To achieve this, it was important to treat the horse in the right way. Because the cowboy had to travel very long distances, he looked for a safe and comfortable way of riding. Both he and his horse had to tire as little as possible. The manner of riding at work, and the games with which the cowboys amused themselves in their free time, are the basis of today's western-style riding.

It is a mistake to suppose that western riding has anything to do with rodeos. Western-style riding is based on simplicity and calm. It could

even be said that western riding most closely resembles dressage.

Western horses

In the past, three breeds have proved their superior suitability for western riding in respect of their characters and musculature: the Quarter horse, the Paint, and the Appaloosa.

Quarter horse
The American Quarter horse is the product of crossing the horses brought to America by the Spaniards with the English horses imported around 1600.

During the seventeenth and eighteenth centuries, horse racing was tremendously popular in America. However, since there were few race courses and scarcely any long straight roads, races were held over short distances in the main street. The distance was rarely more than a quarter of a mile (approximately 400m). Because these horses were faster than any others over this distance, they became known as Quarter horses.

Quarter horses are very versatile and highly intelligent, and generally have excellent temperaments. They are 15 hands high, short coupled, with exceptionally well-muscled quarters and inner hind legs.
The head is small, with a broad forehead, deep jawline, and big, expressive eyes. All solid colours are recognized.

Paint
Paints are Quarter horses with white markings on their bodies above the knee. This distinct breed, with its own register, was created because these horses could not be registered as Quarter horses.

Occasionally, two solid-coated parents would produce a broken-coated foal. It was in order to be able to register these horses somewhere,

Paint

Appaloosa (blanket)

that the American Paint Horse Association was established. (The Paint should not be confused with a pinto, which is a coloured horse of any breed.)

Appaloosa
The name Appaloosa derives from the area where this breed originated: the Palouse river valley in the northern United States.

The colourful horses bred in this area by the Nez-Perce Indians were known as Palouse horses. The current Appaloosas are the product of crossing Palouse horses with Quarter horses.

Appaloosas have tremendous stamina and are both hardy and calm. The most remarkable aspect of the Appaloosa is its colour, which is divided into the following categories:

- Leopard: predominantly white with dark spots over the whole body
- Few-spot: predominantly white with just a few dark spots
- Snowflake: predominantly dark with light spots over the whole body
- Blanket: dark with a white "blanket" on the quarters, with or without spots
- Roan: dark coat flecked with white, with or without "blanket."

Western riding

The basic paces used in western riding are the walk, the jog (resembling a slow trot), and the lope, a slow, smooth canter. A good western-style rider sits naturally in the saddle, with stirrups long enough to enable his legs to hang straight down. The rider's heels are turned slightly outwards, and the toes of his boots point forwards. The rider keeps his back straight and his seat far back in the saddle.

The handling of the reins is particularly characteristic: the reins are very long, and there is a pronounced loop between the hand and the horse's mouth.

In the case of young horses (up to five years old) the reins, which are not buckled together, are held in a loop between both hands. In the

The lope

case of older horses (six years old and over) the reins are held in one hand.

To turn the horse in a given direction, the reins are brought against the right or left side of its neck. In contrast to many other styles of riding, in western riding the horse's head and neck must remain straight between the reins.

The aids are given very lightly, and a good western rider never or hardly ever uses his spurs. Another characteristic of western riding is the halt using the voice: Whoa . . . !

Right: To turn the horse in a given direction, the reins are brought against the right or left side of the neck.

Another characteristic of western riding is the halt using the voice. Whoa . . . !

The most noticeable piece of equipment is the western saddle with its horn, that is put on a folded blanket (pad)

Tack and clothing

The most noticeable piece of equipment is the western saddle with its horn, that is put on a folded blanket (pad). The bridle usually has no noseband. The clothing that has become identified with western riding includes jeans, boots, and a cowboy hat.

Western riding as competitive sport

Western riding competitions can broadly be divided into four types: in-hand showing, dressage, racing, and working. Almost all competitions have junior classes (for horses under five) and senior classes (for horses six and over).

In-hand showing

In these classes, also known as halter classes, the horses are judged in hand. The horse is judged on its paces in walk and trot, its confor-mation, and its behaviour.

These classes are divided according to age and sex.

Showmanship

In this competition the judges consider the skill of the exhibitor rather than the merits of the horse itself. They look at the way the horse has been turned out, and whether the exhibitor is able to show it to its best advantage.

Dressage

Western-style dressage is divided into five sections: western pleasure, western horse-manship, western riding, trail, and reining.

The free hand should touch neither the horse nor the saddle

Western pleasure

A good western pleasure horse should live up to this title - it should be a pleasure to ride. The competitors ride in the arena together and need to show the walk, jog, and lope on both reins. The riders must hold the reins in one hand, and may not change hands. The free hand should touch neither the saddle nor the horse. The judges look for whether the horse behaves calmly, and whether it reacts promptly to the rider's aids.

Western horsemanship

Western horsemanship classes judge the position and skill of the rider, riding with a western saddle and bridle.

A western horsemanship class has two elements: an individual and a group test. In the individual test the rider has to ride a course he has been given in advance. In the group

element of the class, all the competitors show their horses in walk, jog, and lope. The judges look for the position of the riders and the overall impression they create, as well as the way they give their horses the aids.

Western riding
In this class the competitors have to ride a test over a prescribed course which tests the skills of a ranch horse. For example, the test may include riding over a plank and changes of leg at the canter while weaving through a series of obstacles.

At the end of the test, the competitors perform a canter-to-halt transition, followed by a rein back.

Trail

In trail classes the course consists of a number of obstacles that a rider might expect to encounter when riding a trail.

Examples include a gate that has to be opened and shut, planks laid out in an L-shape which the horse and rider have to negotiate backwards, planks they have to cross sideways, and a wooden bridge.

Reining
In reining tests, the rider must show that he has total control over all the horse's movements. The tests require stops, spins, rollbacks, changes of leg, and canter circles.

In reining tests, the rider must show that he has total control over all the horse's movements

Above: Planks which the horse and rider have to cross sideways

Preceding page: In western horsemanship classes the position and skill of the rider are judged

Canter circles are one element of reining tests

Races

Two very popular speed competitions take place nationally and internationally: barrel racing and pole bending.

Barrel racing

In barrel racing, three barrels are placed in a triangle. Competitors must ride a complete circle around each barrel, and the fastest to do so is the winner.

Competitors may touch the barrels, but if they knock one down, a penalty of five seconds is added to their score.

In cutting competitions, horse and rider separate one cow from a herd and drive it to the centre of the arena. The cow may not rejoin the herd

Preceding page: Pole bending

Pole bending

This competition also tests the horse's speed and agility. Six poles are placed in a straight line approximately 7m (23ft) apart. Horse and rider race first to the furthest pole, then return zig-zagging between the poles. They then zig-zag back to the end, before racing past the poles to the finish. Knocking a pole down attracts a five-second penalty.

Working

Western-style riding is seen at its best when horse and rider are driving cattle. Working classes are divided into two sections: working cowhorse and cutting.

Working cowhorse

In this part of the competition, the horse has to show itself capable of working on a ranch. The horse must have not only reining-skill but also cow-sense. Cow-sense is the ability to think and move faster than a cow.

The competition has two parts: dry work (without cattle), which amounts to a reining test, and fence work, the real work with cattle. For this last section a cow is brought into the arena. The horse first has to keep the cow under control at the short side of the arena, before driving it at least twice along the long side, making the cow turn towards the wall before reaching the short side.

Finally, the horse has to drive the cow to the centre of the arena and circle around it once in both directions.

Cutting

In cutting competitions, horse and rider have to separate one cow from a herd and drive it to the centre of the arena. The cow may not rejoin the herd.

CHAPTER 10

Hacking out

Few things are more enjoyable than riding through the countryside on bridle paths. There are, however, quite a few potential snags. You need to be aware of how the horse will behave in the open countryside, you need to know the traffic regulations, and in some countries you need to pass a riding test before you are allowed to hack out.

Hacking out

Hacking out is very different from riding in a school or other enclosed space. Most horses also behave differently outdoors than in a school. They are often more temperamental and may take fright at unexpected situations. A novice rider should not go out alone at first. Horses are calmer and easier to ride in a group. You should ride out alone only when you are fully in control of your horse.

All sorts of different hacks are possible. Some riders enjoy walking through the countryside, so they can observe the beauties of nature at their leisure.

Other riders prefer to travel at a faster pace, covering greater distances. When riding at a greater speed, the horse should never become exhausted. The speed at which a horse can be ridden depends on its physical fitness, strength and endurance, and the nature of the terrain. A horse will tire less quickly on smooth going than on rough. Cantering in loose sand is also demanding for a horse.

Avoid metalled roads as much as possible. Never canter on a metalled road, and only trot in an emergency. Because these roads have no "give" in them, they take their toll of horses' legs.

During a ride, a horse may tense its back and try to stretch its legs. This may be an indication that the horse needs to pass water. In order to let it do so, it is best to stop and stand up in the stirrups, leaning forward in order to relieve the horse's back somewhat.
If you fail to do this, the horse may retain its urine too long and get colic, which is very painful.

Always walk on metalled roads; cantering demands too much from the horse's legs

Above: Before asking a horse to enter unfamiliar water, you should first check to see if the bottom is too soft

Below: Going uphill

Obstacles in the terrain

Going uphill, bend your upper body forwards, supporting yourself with your knees. Make sure you do not interfere with the horse's mouth and, if the hill is very steep, take hold of its mane.

Going downhill, allow the horse to stretch its neck as much as possible. Try to lighten your seat; to descend a steep slope, the horse needs to make full use of its back and quarters. Lean forward so that you can see the slope and steer the horse as necessary.
In most cases you should descend a slope slowly.

When wading through fast-moving water, it is advisable to ride diagonally upstream.

Resting

During a long ride, you should let your horse have a rest. Make sure that you have walked the horse dry. Sweating horses easily catch cold when standing still. Never stand your horse in the wind. If there is no shelter, turn its quarters into the wind. The tail will then afford the horse some protection.

Dress

When hacking out, riders can wear whatever clothes they feel most comfortable in. However, on long rides jodhpurs and riding boots are preferable. It is advisable to wear a hard hat for safety.

Traffic regulations

Many riders will ride out onto the public highway. They then become part of the traffic, and horses and riders count as slow-moving traffic. The following traffic rules generally apply:

Opposite: During a long break, if possible, take the saddle and bridle off and let the horse graze in a headcollar

Right: When riding at dusk or in the dark, make sure you are clearly visible from all directions

- Riders should give way to motor vehicles.
- Riders should ride on the same side of the road as the rest of the traffic.
- Riders are forbidden to use motorways.
- Riders should not ride on paths intended for pedestrians or bicycles.
- Traffic signs for horse-drawn vehicles and cattle also apply to riders.
- From dusk to dawn, in fog, heavy snow, or any other conditions of poor visibility, riders should carry a light which is white in front and red behind.

Although riders should ride on the same side of the road as other road users, the exception is if

the verge on the other side of the road is large and more suitable.

Bridleways

Usually you are not permitted to ride across country at will. Riders are normally confined to bridleways and other rights of way.

Riders using bridleways should obey certain rules in respect of other users. A rider wishing to overtake another rider should approach them in walk. Having caught their attention, he should then ask if he may pass.

Passing a rider coming in the other direction should also be done in walk.

When you are riding with a group and wish to cross a road, the whole group should cross together, not following nose to tail, otherwise you would hold up the traffic too much

In those places where you may ride freely across country, never ride on fields of crops.

Riding and driving tests

In some countries, riders and those driving horse-drawn vehicles outside a riding school are required to have passed a test, and must carry a pass to prove it. Those in possession of such a pass frequently attract better insurance rates.

Riding test

In the Netherlands, this test involves a theoretical and a practical examination. The theoretical element consists of a multiple-choice paper covering the care of the horse, knowledge about saddlery, traffic regulations, and riding etiquette

In the practical examination the rider needs to show that he has a good riding position and can control a horse in walk, trot, and canter. He also needs to show that he can mount and dismount correctly.

To pass the horse-driving test in the Netherlands, you need to demonstrate that you are able to drive a horse on the public highway

Horse-driving test

In the Netherlands, the theoretical element of this test is largely the same as that for riders, with the addition of questions about driving. For the practical part of the test, a candidate needs to be able to tack up and harness a horse correctly to a vehicle, to mount and dismount the box safely and correctly, and to drive a horse up to the bit in walk and trot during a half-hour road test. This test takes place on the public highway with other traffic.

The examiner is looking for, among other things, the ability to drive with a still hand, control of the whip, obedience to traffic regulations, and control of the horse in unexpected situations.

Health and sickness

This last chapter focuses on how to recognize a healthy horse and, what is perhaps even more important, how to recognize when your horse is sick, and how to treat possible injuries.

Right: After giving birth the mare licks the foal all over

Below: A healthy horse takes an interest in its environment

A healthy horse

If you keep a horse, or if you intend to buy one, you must know what the signs of a healthy horse are:

- A healthy horse has a lively look in its eye and takes an interest in its surroundings.
- The normal temperature of a horse varies between 37.5 and 38.5°C.
- The body is uniformly warm. Only the ears and the lower legs feel a little colder.
- The mucous membranes of its nose, mouth, and eyes are pink and moist.
- The horse eats well. (If a horse leaves its feed, first check that the feed is not mouldy or otherwise unpalatable.)
- Breathing is steady and rhythmic, between 9 and 15 inhalations per minute when the horse is at rest.
- The horse passes large amounts of droppings without difficulty. Depending on the feed, droppings may vary in consistency and in colour, from green to dark brown.
- The coat is smooth and glossy.
- The horse walks steadily and firmly.

If you think your horse is not quite well, it is a good idea to take its temperature

This horse has grease (also known as grapes). Grease is an infection that occurs most frequently in horses out at grass in the wet

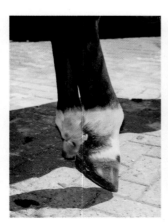

The wound is first dried thoroughly . . .

. . . and then dressed with a special ointment

This horse has a serious case of grease so the infection is bandaged and the horse stabled for three days

A sick horse

You should of course not only know what a healthy horse looks like, but you should also be able to determine whether a horse is sick. The following symptoms may indicate that all is not well with the horse:

- The horse is listless. It hangs its head, its ears are motionless, and it has no interest in its surroundings.
- The horse has a high temperature.
- The body is not uniformly warm, and the ears and lower legs feel either hot or very cold.
- The mucous membranes of its nose, mouth, and eyes are pale, dark red or yellow, and dry.
- The horse has gone off its food.
- Breathing is irregular, or jerky, and occurs with very noticeable movement of the nostrils or flanks.
- There is a whistling sound with each intake of breath.
- The horse has a dry cough.
- Droppings are small, hard and dark in colour, or very soft and watery.
- The horse keeps lying down and getting up again (which indicates colic).
- The horse is unwilling to move, or walks unsteadily and painfully, or by weaving from side to side.
- The coat is dull and staring.

The foal has a bad cough and a runny nose. In order to find out what is the matter, the veterinarian listens to its breathing

The veterinarian takes its temperature . . .

. . . and looks at the colour of its mucous membranes

The veterinarian diagnoses that the foal has pneumonia. She gives it an injection in a blood vessel to bring down its temperature . . .

. . . and she gives it antibiotics to fight the bacteria

The nature of the illness and the experience of the person caring for the horse determine whether or not a veterinarian should be called. An inexperienced person will have more difficulty determining whether or not the case is serious than someone who has been looking after horses for many years. The golden rule where veterinarians is concerned is: better twice for nothing than once too late.

The first aid kit

When putting together a first aid kit for the stable, you need to ask yourself what could go wrong with a horse and what you could responsibly do about it. A good pair of hands and eyes are the most important. Always look and feel your horse over thoroughly when grooming it. Keep an eye open for unusual behaviour, swellings, painful areas, and heat. A thermometer is very helpful if you suspect that something may be wrong.

Injuries from all sorts of causes are the most frequent occurrence: bruises, surface cuts, and deep wounds which may have damaged tendons or bones. Arnica (in the form of a pill under the tongue) can be most helpful in the case of bruises from knocks, falls, or kicks. Surface wounds are best treated by cleaning them and spraying the area with an antiseptic spray. It is best to call a veterinarian for deep wounds. Never spray disinfectant straight into a wound! Disinfectant not only kills the bacteria, it also breaks down tissue cells, which

It is usually a good idea to bandage bruises

To avoid equine flu, it is advisable to inoculate the horse against it twice a year

then become a breeding ground for new bacteria. Even washing a wound with tap water may damage the tissue cells.

It is a good idea to worm your horse regularly. If the horse is always in the same field, you should do this every six to eight weeks. Keeping worming powders in the first aid box may ensure that you do not forget to do so.

Finally, do not collect a large array of potions and lotions. They are usually out of date by the time you need them.

It is not always easy to choose the right remedy for a particular problem. Never hesitate to ask your veterinarian or another specialist for advice.

An open wound with "proud" flesh. In order to speed up the healing process, the veterinarian will need to cut it out regularly

A syringe for administering worming paste

If everything goes well at a birth, the mare will do it all on her own. If the foal is presented correctly, the forelegs will emerge first, followed by the head

Index

Photo credits

Natasha Bruinsma: p.7, 9l, 11r, 34.
Jan Kan: p.5, 13 ar, 13br, 26, 32b, 76.
Jacob Melissen: p.9r, 11a, 12, 14, 15r, 16, 19, 20, 22b, 23, 24, 25, 27, 30, 31, 32a, 33, 35, 36, 37a, 37b, 46, 47, 77, 78, 79a, 81, 82b, 83, 84, 85, 88, 89, 90, 91, 92b, 93, 94, 95, 97, 98al, 98ar, 98, 99, 99al, 99ar, 101, 106, 108, 109, 110a, 110b, 111, 112, 113, 117b, 127, 128, 137, 141b, 142, 143.
Cees Versteeg: p.4, 8, 15l, 17, 21, 22a, 28, 29, 38, 39, 40l, 40r, 41, 42b, 42a, 43, 44, 45, 48a, 48m, 48b, 49l, 49r, 50a, 50b, 51al, 51ar, 51bl, 51br, 52al, 52ar, 52bl, 52br, 53al, 53ar, 53bl, 53br, 54a, 54b, 55a, 55b, 56l, 57, 58, 59a, 59b, 60, 61, 62al, 62bl, 62ar, 62br, 63, 64, 66l, 67, 68, 69, 70l, 70r, 71al, 71ar, 71b, 72b, 73a, 73b, 74al, 74ar, 74bl, 74br, 75a, 75b, 79b, 80a, 80b, 82a, 86al, 86ar, 86b, 87, 92ar, 92al, 96al, 96ml, 96bl, 96ar, 96mr, 96br, 100, 102ar, 102mr, 102br, 103, 104a, 104b, 105ar, 105bl, 105br, 107l, 107r, 114, 115a, 115b, 117a, 120a, 120b, 123bl, 126, 129ar, 129br, 130, 131, 132, 133, 134, 135, 136, 138a, 138bl, 138bm, 138br, 139ar, 139bl 139bm, 139br, 140l, 140r, 141a, 141m.
Peter Wassing: p.116, 118, 119, 121, 122, 123al, 123r, 124, 125.

Acknowledgements

With thanks to the following businesses, organizations and people for their co-operation and advice:

Femke Dijkstra, Manege
    de Nieuwe Heuvel,
    Lunteren
Irmgard Geul, Nedpoint
    Quarterhorses,
    Leusden
Burgmeyer Quarterhorses,
    Vorstenbosch
Heja, the saddlery and
    horse trailers,
    Garderen
Federatiecentrum, Ermelo
Zadelmakerij Gebroeders
    van der Wiel N.V.
Manege de Galgenbergh,
    Garderen
Arthur's Western Store,
    Vorstenbosch
Western Store, The
    Western Import
    Company, Rijswijk
Hoefsmid Jan de Zwaan,
    Hierden
Dierenarts Ellen Kral,
    Paardenkliniek de
    Veluwe, Vierhouten

Dierenarts John Pijnappel,
    Nijmegen
Rij-instructrice Yvonne
    Schute, Garderen
Bert Wiekema, Western
    Ruiter Associatie
    Nederland
Bert van Veen, Reint
    Knoppert and Irene
    Helsdingen
Jan and Ankie van den
    Brink
Geesje van Nunen
Claudia Boon
Nelleke Dijkhuizen
Anouschka van Hierden
Ginny Rozema
Christel Jongboer
Mireille and Willem van
    Someren
Harry Kock, Peter
    Kuijssen, Henk
    Hermsen and Fred
    Schutte

and many others.